Quick Rick

Rick can run. He likes to sprint.

I like running! I am quick as a flash!
Zip!

Zip!
Zip!
Zip!

Rick bumps into Tom and his little, brown dog, Fuzz.

I am so quick. I am quicker than a car!
Lick! Lick!
Wag! Wag!

Rick and Tom do not see Bad Val.
Bad Val grabs Fuzz!

Come back, you crook! Fuzz is **my** dog!
Help!

Rick is quick. He will get Bad Val.

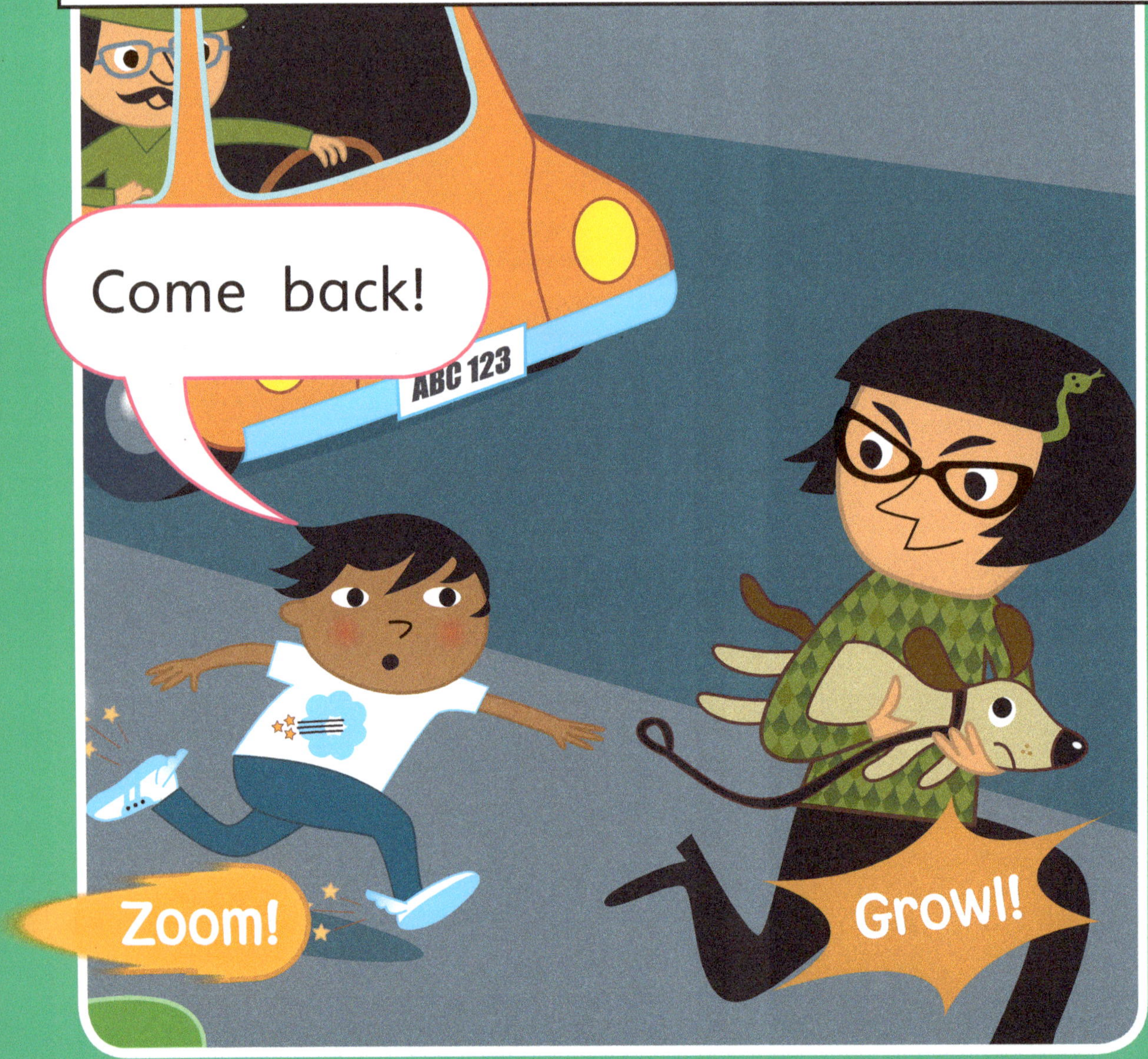
Come back!
ABC 123
Zoom!
Growl!

Val jumps into a car.
Zoom!
I can get that car!

Val springs onto a train.
I can stop that train!

Bad Val spots a jet.
I will get that jet!
Sob!
Zoom!
I miss Fuzz.

Rick will not stop me!

Rick bursts in. He turns off the jet.

On
Off
Splutter!
Splutter!

Bad Val can not get out.

Rick has got Fuzz and Bad Val.

You are too quick for me!
Ruff!
Ruff!

There you are, little one!
Ruff! Ruff!
Now Bad Val will have to go to jail!
Clink!
I do not like this!